God is Good

God Made

# the

# Opossum

By Mrs. James Swartzentruber

Pictures by Daniel Zook and Lester Miller

**To the Teacher:**

This book is designed to give constructive reading practice to pupils using the grade one *Bible Nurture and Reader Series.* It uses words that have been introduced in the reader or can be mastered with phonics skills taught by Unit 4, Lesson 5. A few new words also appear in the story, printed in italics. At the end of the book, these words are listed with pronunciations and / or illustrations to help the children to learn them on their own. Be sure the children understand that the words are vocabulary or sound words except the words in italics, and where to look to learn the new words if they need help. They should be able to read this book independently.

Books in this series with their placement according to reading and phonics lessons:

*Copyright, 1976*
By
**Rod and Staff Publishers, Inc.**
**Crockett, Kentucky 41413**
**Telephone (606) 522-4348**
Printed in U.S.A.

ISBN 0-7399-0064-1
Catalog no. 2256

13    14    15    16    —    15    14    13    12    11    10    09

"There, done at last! That surely is a warm job on a day like this!"

Glen was tired. He walked

over to a nice, big shade tree. "Oh, that cool air feels good!"

He propped the hoe on the tree and wiped the *sweat* from his face. "I think I will rest a little and cool off a bit," he *thought*.

Glen sat down on the grass and leaned on the tree. "It surely is a nice day," he *thought*, sitting there and looking around him. "The sky is so blue. A few white clouds—"

Thud!

Glen jumped. "What was that?"

There lay a little gray animal beside Glen. He jumped up to run away. He did not know what kind of animal it was. But seeing that it did not move, he did not run.

It lay very still.

"It looks as if it were *dead*," said Glen to himself. Pushing it with his *shoe*, he said. "It surely is *dead*."

"But where did it come from?" Glen looked up into the tree. "It must have been up there."

"I will go and find Andrew. Maybe he will know what it is."

But where was Andrew? He had been helping Father in the shop. Maybe he was still there. But Andrew was not in the shop. Would he be in the barn?

Running to the barn, Glen called, "Andrew! Andrew!"

He opened the *door* and went inside. "Andrew! Andrew!" he called. "Where are you?"

Everything was quiet. Andrew was not there.

"Maybe Mother will know where Andrew is," *thought* Glen, running to the house.

But before he got to the house, he saw Andrew picking cherries in the tree behind the house. "Andrew!" he called.

"What?" asked Andrew, looking down at his brother.

"I want to show you something."

"I am just about finished up here. Then I will come. What is it?"

"I don't know. I *thought* maybe you would know. I was sitting under the tree out by the corncrib, and a little animal fell down beside me. I never saw anything like it."

"Is it still there?"

"Yes. It was *dead*."

"*Dead*?" asked Andrew.

"Yes. I don't know why it would have been *dead* in the tree. It must have died up there and fell down. I think I will come up and help you."

"I just need a few more," said
Andrew. "But you may help. If
the animal is *dead*, it will not run
away."

"These look good," said Glen
picking a handful of nice, ripe, red
cherries. He popped them into his
mouth. "And they are good!" he
said.

"I *thought* you said you want to help me." Andrew said with a smile.

"I will now." Glen smiled, too.

"This is all we need," said Andrew. "Mother said she wanted this pail full. I will take these in to Mother; then I will

come out to the tree to see what you have found."

Glen ran out to the tree. He looked for the little gray animal. Where was it? He looked all around. It was not there!

Andrew saw Glen looking around. "Isn't it there anymore?" he asked.

"No, it was right there," Glen said, pointing to the place where it had lain. "I was sitting here by the tree and it fell right here."

He bent down to look closer. "See, you can see where it lay."

Andrew looked. "You are right," he said. "But maybe it was not *dead* after all."

"I am sure it was," said Glen. "It looked very *dead*. Its mouth was even hanging open."

"Do you think Father might know what it was?" asked Andrew. "Let's ask him when he comes home. Grandfather wanted him to help him a little. I think he will soon be back."

Glen saw a car coming down the road. "There he comes now!" he cried, running to meet him.

"Father," said Glen, "I was sitting out under the tree by the corncrib when I finished the hoeing this morning. All at once a little animal fell beside me. It was *dead*. But Andrew and I went out to see it, and it is not there anymore."

"Oh, Glen," said Andrew, "maybe Fritz took it away somewhere."

"Oh," said Glen. He had not *thought* about that.

"Tell me more about the animal," said Father. "How did it look?"

"It had a long, pointed nose and a thin tail like a rat's tail," Glen said.

"Was it gray?" asked Father. "And did it have black feet and white toes? And did the ears not have any hair on them?"

"I do not remember all of that," said Glen, "but it was gray."

"Are you sure it was *dead*?" asked Father.

"Yes, its mouth was even hanging open. I took my *shoe* and kicked it, and it did not move at all."

Father smiled. "I can guess what you saw, and I doubt that Fritz took it away," he said.

"What was it, Father?" asked Glen and Andrew at the same time.

"I think you saw an *opossum.* I do not know why it fell out of the tree. Maybe it played *dead* up in the tree when it saw you and then fell. Or maybe it slipped and fell and then played *dead.*"

"You mean it was not *dead* at all?" asked Glen. "But why would it play *dead*?"

"God made the *opossum* to do that," said Father. "When people or animals come near, it acts as if it were *dead* so that they will not do anything to it.

"When people and animals see it, they think it is *dead* and leave it alone. Then they go away.

"When the *opossum* thinks it is safe to do so, it goes away, too."

"I wish I would have been really quiet for a long time," said Glen. "Maybe I could have watched it get up and walk away."

"But *opossums* don't live in trees, do they?" asked Andrew.

"No, but they do get food in trees sometimes," said Father. "They like to eat eggs. Where it is hard to get into the nests, they can wrap their tails around a limb and eat right out of the nest, hanging by their tails above it!"

"So that is what was going on!" cried Glen. "When I was hoeing, the birds were flying around and scolding. I could not see any cat or any other thing that would make them act like that."

"The mother *opossum* has a pouch where the little ones stay for about 8 weeks after they are born," Father went on to say. "When baby *opossums* are born, they are so little that you could put about 15 or 20 in a teaspoon."

"They must be very little!"
cried Glen.

"Yes, they are," said Father. "When we see how God made everything, it helps us to understand what a great and wonderful God we have. Everything He made and does is very good."

thought (thôt)

opossum (o·pos·um)

sweat (swet)

dead (ded)

shoe (sho͞o)

door (dôr)